Rocks and Minerals

Gail Tuchman

SCHOLASTIC INC.

New York Toronto London Auckland
Sydney Mexico City New Delhi Hong Kong

P9-DCQ-069

Read more! Do more!

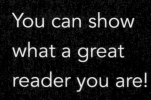

After you read this book, download your free all-new digital activities.

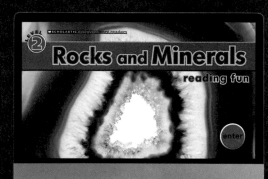

You can show what a great reader you are!

For Mac and PC

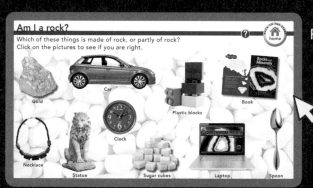

Take quizzes about the fun facts in this book!

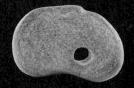

Do fun activities with simple step-by-step instructions!

Log on to

www.scholastic.com/discovermore/readers

Enter this special code: **L2D3MGJFX7P2**

2

Contents

ISBN 978-0-545-83947-1

12 11 10 9 8 7 6 5 4 3 2 1   15 16 17 18 19 20/0

Printed in the U.S.A.   40
This edition first printing, September 2015

Scholastic is constantly working to lessen the environmental
impact of our manufacturing processes. To view our
industry-leading paper procurement policy,
visit www.scholastic.com/paperpolicy.

Our rocky Earth

Look at this crystal cave! This cave that two miners found in Mexico is amazing. The cave is filled with GIANT 500,000-year-old rock crystals. Some are 36 feet long and weigh over 50 tons!

Rocks tell stories of our planet. They tell of its changes over time. Geologists study rocks to read Earth's stories.

NEW WORD

geologist
jee-AH-luh-jist
A **geologist** is a scientist who studies rocks and minerals.

SAY IT OUT LOUD

Did you ever bite into a piece of chocolate and find a tasty surprise inside? On the outside, a geode (a hollow rock) looks plain. Break it open. It might have a surprise center! Inside the rock, sparkling white and purple mineral crystals have formed. Most rocks are made of a mix of minerals. Minerals form into shapes called crystals.

A geode has a plain outside.

Geode

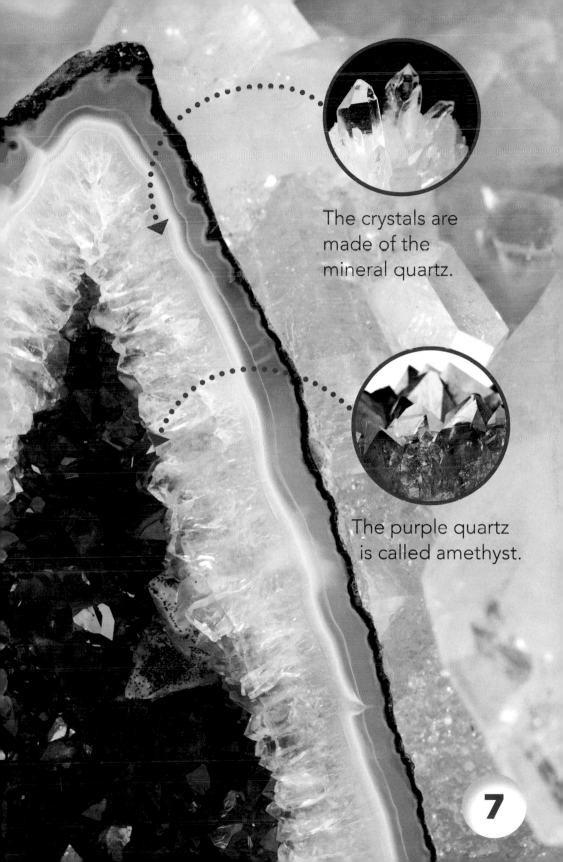

The crystals are made of the mineral quartz.

The purple quartz is called amethyst.

Sparkling gems

Some minerals are cut and polished. They become beautiful gems. Gems can be made into jewelry. Diamonds shine. Rubies, sapphires, and emeralds burst with bright colors. These precious gems are hard to find.

Uncut diamonds

This ring has a beautiful cut and polished diamond.

Emeralds

Rubies

Peridots

Quartz

Topaz

Garnets

Opal

Sapphires

Aquamarines

9

There is a gem for the month of the year that you were born in. This is called a birthstone. Long ago, people thought that birthstones brought good health and good luck.

Dr. Raquel Alonso-Perez has a sparkly job at a museum. She looks after gems: "I ask kids about their birthdays. For a February birthday, I show my favorite gem, amethyst. It is a purple quartz—one of the most common minerals on Earth!"

Amethyst

Which is your birthstone?

January	February	March
Garnet	**Amethyst**	**Aquamarine**
April	**May**	**June**
Diamond	**Emerald**	**Pearl**
July	**August**	**September**
Ruby	**Peridot**	**Sapphire**
October	**November**	**December**
Opal	**Topaz**	**Turquoise**

Planet rock

Our planet formed 4.6 billion years ago. It is made up of layers. We live on the crust—the hard, rocky outer layer. Inside Earth is very hot rock.

Hard outer layer

Hot inner layers

It's a fact!

The deepest hole ever dug into

There are three main groups of rocks:

Igneous rock

Sedimentary rock

Metamorphic rock

Earth's crust is 7.6 miles deep.

Igneous rocks

Deep inside Earth, fiery heat melts rocks into a liquid called magma. When it erupts from a volcano, it is called lava. Above the ground, the lava quickly cools and hardens into new igneous rock. The new rock is basalt.

Kilauea volcano erupts in Hawaii. A red-hot river of lava oozes down the slopes. The temperature of the lava is 2,100°F!

NEW WORD

igneous rock
IG-nee-uhs rahk
Granite and basalt are the most common **igneous rocks**.

SAY IT OUT LOUD

Basalt has small crystals.

15

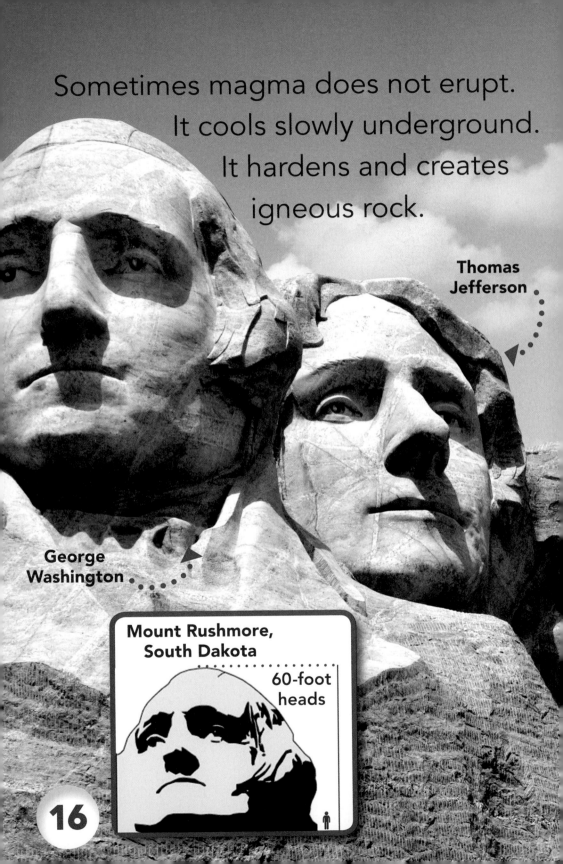

Sometimes magma does not erupt.
It cools slowly underground.
It hardens and creates
igneous rock.

Thomas
Jefferson

George
Washington

**Mount Rushmore,
South Dakota**

60-foot
heads

This monument of US presidents was carved into a granite mountain. Granite is hard and strong. It took 400 people and 14 years to complete the monument.

Granite has large crystals.

Theodore Roosevelt

Abraham Lincoln

Sedimentary rocks

Wind, water, and ice break rocks into small bits. These bits, called sediment, wash into lakes and oceans. Sediment piles up in layers. Over time, the layers press together to form new rock.

This rock in Arizona, the Wave, is carved by the wind. It is colored by minerals. Bands of reds, pinks, and yellows ripple through the sandstone.

NEW WORD

sedimentary rock

sed-uh-MEN-tur-ee rahk

The bottom layers of **sedimentary rock** are the oldest.

SAY IT OUT LOUD

Sometimes you can find leaf prints or even dinosaur bones in sedimentary rock. The remains of plants or animals held in rocks are called fossils.

HOW A FOSSIL FORMS

1. A dinosaur leaves footprints in soft mud.

2. The footprints are covered by sand or other sediment.

Fossils tell of life on Earth in the past. Ammonites swam in the seas over 200 million years ago. You might find an ammonite fossil on land.

Ammonite

3. Over time, the footprints turn to stone with the sediment.

4. Earth's changes slowly uncover the fossil.

Metamorphic rocks

Cookie dough changes into cookies when it's baked. Like the dough, rocks deep inside Earth are "baked" and squeezed. The great heat and

Limestone becomes *marble*.

Sedimentary limestone

Metamorphic marble

pressure change igneous and sedimentary rocks. They turn into metamorphic rocks.

Shale becomes slate.

Sedimentary shale

Metamorphic slate

Using rocks and minerals

Some of the world's most amazing buildings are made of rock. Long ago, ancient Egyptians took stone from pits called quarries. They cut huge blocks by hand to build the Great Pyramid.

Today, people still get building stones from quarries. Now machines help drill, blast, cut, and move rocks.

Marble is cut into blocks from quarry walls.

The blocks are sorted and loaded.

In a factory, the blocks are cut to size.

What things in your life come from rocks and minerals?

Walkways

On a walkway, you may be stepping on a sedimentary rock called bluestone.

Brick walls

Clay is baked at a high temperature. It makes strong brick walls.

Oil

Oil comes from sedimentary rock. It heats homes, powers vehicles, and is made into plastics.

Cars

A car's window glass comes from quartz sand, soda ash, and limestone.

It's a fact!

An average car contains about

Clocks and watches

Vibrating quartz crystals help your clock keep exact time.

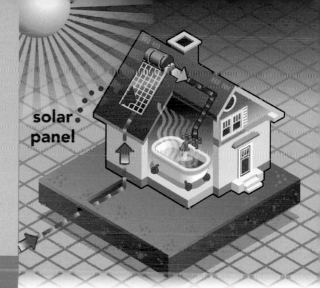

solar panel

Sculptures

The Lincoln Memorial is carved from marble.

Solar panels

Sunlight is changed into electricity using silicon.

Computers

Data is processed by silicon chips.

Curbstone

Tough granite is used to make curbs.

Salt

Salt keeps food from spoiling and adds flavor. It melts ice on roads in winter.

37 different minerals!

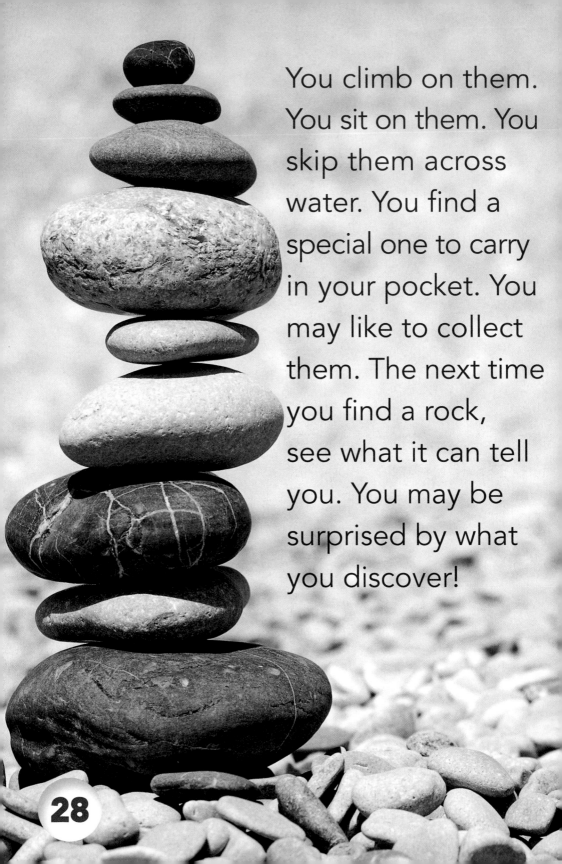

You climb on them. You sit on them. You skip them across water. You find a special one to carry in your pocket. You may like to collect them. The next time you find a rock, see what it can tell you. You may be surprised by what you discover!

Kunzite

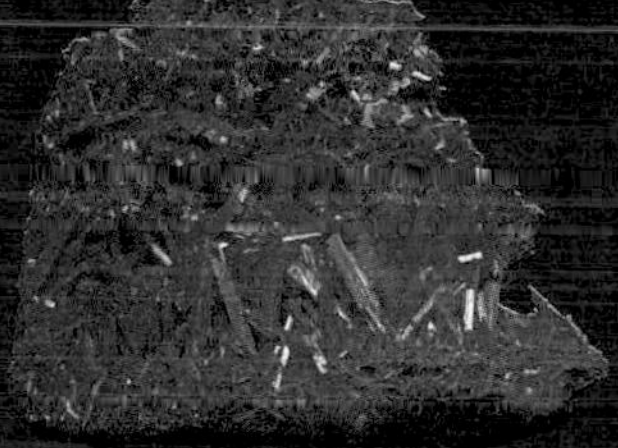

Lead chromate

Tourmaline

Marble

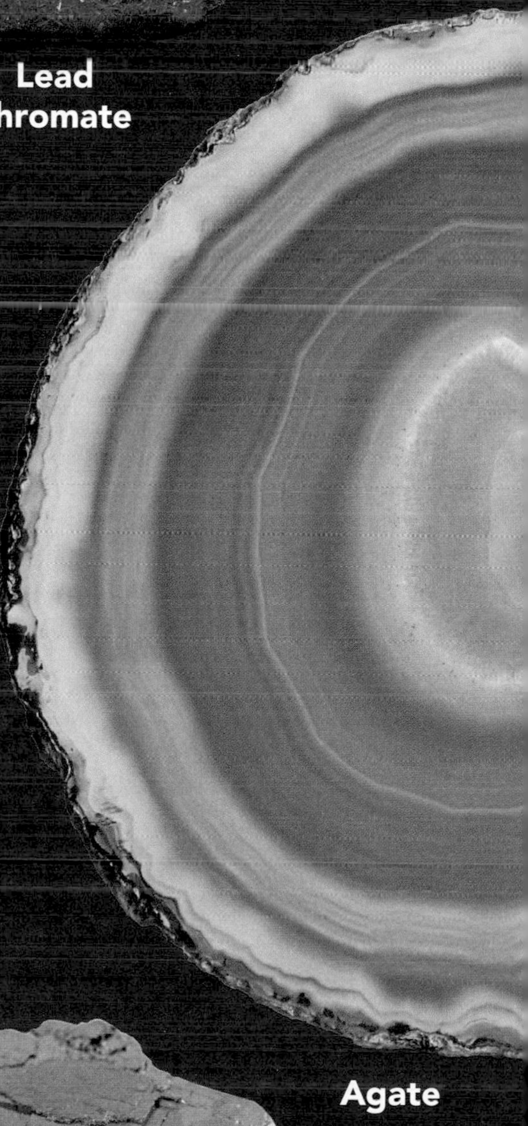

Agate

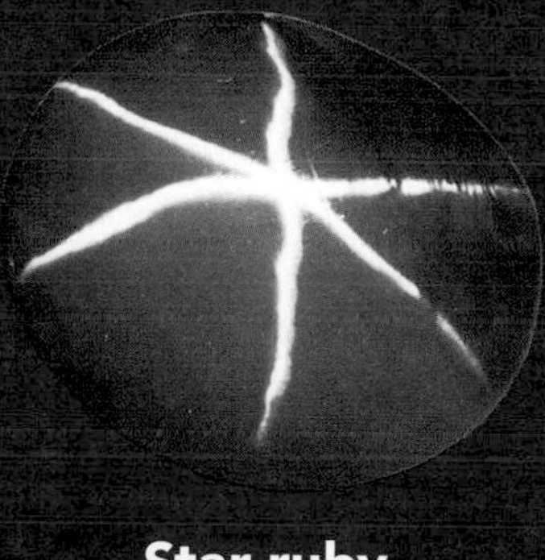

Star ruby

Galena

29

Glossary

ammonite
A sea creature with a spiral shell that died out 65 million years ago.

birthstone
The gem that is connected to the month of your birth.

crust
The hard, rocky outer layer of Earth.

crystal
A solid material with a pattern of flat surfaces. Minerals are formed from crystals.

erupt
To suddenly throw out something, like lava from a volcano.

fossil
A bone, shell, footprint, or other trace of an animal or plant from millions of years ago, preserved as rock.

gem
A precious mineral that has been cut and polished and can be used in jewelry.

geode
A rock with crystals inside it.

geologist
A scientist who studies rocks and minerals.

igneous rock
A rock that forms from cooled magma or lava.

lava
The hot, liquid rock that comes out of a volcano when it erupts.

magma
Melted rock beneath Earth's surface that becomes lava when it flows out of a volcano.

metamorphic rock
A rock that has been changed into a new type of rock by heat and pressure.

miner
A person who digs up minerals from the ground.

mineral
A material from nature that does not come from an animal or plant. Most rocks are made of minerals.

precious
Very valuable.

pressure
The force produced when something is pressed or squeezed.

quarry
A place, often a large hole or pit, where rock is dug from the ground.

rock
A hard material, usually made of one or more minerals, that forms on or under Earth's surface.

sediment
Small pieces of rock, sand, and dirt that are carried away by wind or water and settle on the ground or at the bottoms of rivers, lakes, and oceans.

sedimentary rock
A rock that forms from layers of sediment that have been pressed together.

vibrate
To move back and forth quickly.

volcano
An opening in Earth's crust through which hot, melted rock erupts.

Index

Images

123RF/Chen Yunpeng: 16 bc; Alamy Images: 11 turquoise (Greg C Grace), 8 cl (imageBROKER), 20 t bg, 21 t bg (Peter Cripps), 29 kunzite (The Natural History Museum); American Museum of Natural History/Van Pelt photographers: 29 star ruby; Bridgeman Art Library/Ancient Art and Architecture Collection Ltd.: 24 c drawing; Dreamstime: 6 bl (Agcuesta), 28 (Andriy Bezuglov), 27 cr arrow (Annsunnyday), 24 bg (Chaiyaphong Kitphaephaisan), 27 tl clock (Cherezoff), 12 bg, 13 bg (Dave Bredeson), 16 b bg, 17 b bg (Dreamshot), 24 papyrus (Edwardgerges), 25 iPad image (Felinda), 27 bl granite (Graemo), 8 cr, 9 emeralds, 9 garnet, 9 sapphires (Ingemar Magnusson), 27 cl (Jarnogz), 32 b (Joao Virissimo), 3 b bg (John Pavlish), 27 bl grass (Karakedi74), 26 br car (Kontur-vid), 12 c (Leonello Calvetti), 21 br figure (Leremy), 6 bg, 7 bg (Marcel Clemens), 7 tr (Martin Novak), 2 tl green rock, 29 tourmaline (Miriam Doerr), 26 l bricks (Mrjafari), 2 tl red rock, 2 tl blue rock (Mrreporter), 32 sky (Nicky Jacobs), 13 metamorphic rock (Paul Lemke), 18 b, 19 b (Photoguy707), 26 l rocks (Richard Mcguirk), 24 pyramid (Rixie), 10 bg, 11 bg (Robert Kneschke), 16 t bg, 17 t bg, 18 t bg, 19 t bg (Ron Chapple), 1 (Russell Shively), 25 bg (Sarah-jane Allen), 6 r geode, 7 l geode (Simon Zenger), 14 bg, 15 bg (Slim Sepp), 25 bl (Stevanzz), 22 bg, 23 bg (TMarchev), 11 aquamarine (Travis Manley), 25 bc (Vasilis Ververidis), 8 bg, 9 bg (Victoria Suhanova), 7 cr (Vivilweb); Fotolia: 9 rubies (imfotograf), 29 agate (Kot63), inside front cover silhouette, 13 t silhouette (leremy), 10 tl (nikolafoto21); inside front cover diamonds (Piktoworld), 3 bl man (Rainer Olzem), 13 igneous rock (siloto), 29 galena (Tyler Boyes); iStockphoto: 11 opal (alicat), 13 b silhouettes (AlonzoDesign), 11 diamond (AptTone), 11 sapphire (Arpad Benedek), 27 tr house (aurielaki), 27 cr computer (carbouv), 8 br (CGinspiration), 27 br salt (EasyBuy4u), 10 paper (Electric_Crayon), 11 amethyst (EnlightenedMedia), 27 cr chip (filonmar), 27 br salt (gilas), 2 bl rock (giocalde), 10 br (HansJoachim), 11 ruby (impactimage), 9 peridot, 9 t quartz, 9 b quartz, 9 aquamarine (J-Palys), 22 cl (JustinMcD), 13 sedimentary rock (Liz Leyden), 11 pearl (loops7), 29 lead chromate (MarcelC), cover bg (mariusFM77), 25 br (maskpro), 30 bg, 31 bg (Nastya22), 2 arrows (papadesign), 2 iPads, 25 iPad (Pixsooz), back cover computer, 2 computer (skodonnell), 8 tape, 10 tape, 25 tape (spxChrome), 11 emerald, 11 peridot, 11 topaz (SunChan), 26 tr oil (wittyn11), 20 bl dinosaur (woewchikyury); Raquel Alonso-Perez, PhD: 10 bl; Scholastic Inc.: cover bl, back cover tl (Gary Ombler), 29 marble; Science Source: 17 c inset (Biophoto Associates), 15 c inset (Claude Nuridsany & Marie Perennou), 22 cr, 23 cr (GIPhotoStock), 4 bg, 5 bg (Javier Trueba/MSF), 11 garnet (Joel Arem), cover br, cover cr, 3 cr rock (Mark A. Schneider), 9 topaz, 9 opal (Phil Degginger/Jack Clark Collection), 23 cl (Trevor Clifford Photography); Shutterstock, Inc./Lorelyn Medina: 12 bl cartoon, 26 bl cartoon.